I0796306

ENGINEERING ANSWERS

How Toilets Flush and Fill

BY DONNA B. McKINNEY

An Imprint of Abdo Publishing
abdobooks.com

abdobooks.com

Printed in the United States of America, North Mankato, Minnesota.
102024
012025

Cover Photo: Shutterstock Images
Interior Photos: Shutterstock Images, 4–5, 6, 9, 10, 12–13, 18, 23, 24, 25, 28; Timofey Manzyuk/Shutterstock Images, 15; Michael Marcotte/Alamy, 16; Dorling Kindersley ltd/Alamy, 20–21; Marcel Derweduwen/Shutterstock Images, 26; Andrea Danti/Shutterstock Images, 29

Editor: Marley Richmond
Series Designer: Laura Kuchar

Library of Congress Control Number: 2024938367

Publisher's Cataloging-in-Publication Data

Names: McKinney, Donna B., author.
Title: How toilets flush and fill / by Donna B. McKinney
Description: Minneapolis, Minnesota: ABDO Publishing, 2025 | Series: Engineering answers | Includes online resources and index.
Identifiers: ISBN 9781098295905 (lib. bdg.) | ISBN 9798384916901 (ebook)
Subjects: LCSH: Engineering--Juvenile literature. | Flush toilets--Juvenile literature. | Toilets--History--Juvenile literature. | Sewer design--Juvenile literature. | Questions and answers--Juvenile literature. | Engineering design--Juvenile literature.
Classification: DDC 620.1--dc23

CONTENTS

About one-fourth of the water used in US homes every year is used to flush toilets.

CHAPTER 1

Flush!

Ava wakes up. She heads to the bathroom and sits on the toilet. This is her first stop of the morning as she gets ready for school. She finishes and reaches for the toilet handle. With just a gentle push, the flush begins.

Swirling water helps clean out the toilet bowl while it is flushing.

Water in the toilet bowl swirls. Swoosh! Waste and water flow out of the bowl. They move down pipes toward the **sewer system**.

Fresh water from the toilet tank quickly refills the bowl. The toilet is ready for use again.

The Flush Toilet Arrives

Before flush toilets, people disposed of waste in the streets or in holes. This created a big, stinky problem. In cities, **sewage** spilled onto streets. Soon, this waste flowed into rivers. Sewage made the drinking water unclean. It spread diseases to people.

In the late 1700s and 1800s, inventors improved the design of early toilets. These new toilets could flush. They were similar to the toilets people use today.

The basics of how all flush toilets work are the same. Clean water is stored in a tank.

When the toilet is flushed, a curved pipe carries away water and waste to the sewer system.

Engineers continued to improve flush toilets. Tanks were once built on the wall above the toilet. Then engineers designed a water tank attached to the bowl. Now toilets take up less space. Inventors also improved the toilet's flush system so toilets do not **clog** easily.

A Queen's Toilet

Sir John Harington invented an early version of a flush toilet in the 1590s. Water ran through this toilet to push waste down a pipe. Harington made one of these toilets for Queen Elizabeth I of England. Inventors did not improve on Harington's design for about 200 years.

Sewer systems bring waste to treatment plants. There, solid waste is removed. The water is cleaned to be used again.

A toilet is a simple device. But its work is very important. Today, homes, schools, and businesses all have toilets.

Some problems with toilets, such as clogs, are easy for people to fix on their own. Plumbers can fix more complicated problems.

Flush toilets safely carry away waste. Homes and public spaces stay clean. This helps keep people healthy.

Primary Source

A writer for the Science Museum in London, England, explained how sewers were built to deal with waste from early flush toilets:

> It involved replacing or upgrading much of the existing . . . system and constructing around 1,100 miles [1770 km] of new sewers. . . . [The waste] was dumped into the Thames, to be carried out with the tide.

Source: "Flushed Away." *Science Museum*, 2 Feb. 2021, sciencemuseum.org.uk. Accessed 15 May 2024.

What's the Big Idea?

Read this quote carefully. What is its main idea? Explain how the main idea is supported by details.

Toilet seats should
be cleaned regularly.

CHAPTER 2

Washing Away Waste

A toilet has many parts that work together to flush away waste. The toilet bowl has a round shape, similar to an upside-down bell. A lid covers the bowl. The lid can be opened and closed. The bowl has a ring-shaped seat.

This seat can be raised or lowered. The bowl and the tank hold clean water.

At the bottom of the bowl is the trap. The trap is a pipe shaped like an S or a P. The trap keeps out the bad smells from the sewer system below. It also keeps water inside the bowl. When a toilet is flushed, water and waste travel through the trap. Most toilets flush waste into a sewer system.

Powerful Public Toilets

Toilets in public spaces, such as schools or businesses, get lots of use. They are more powerful than home toilets. Most public toilets do not have tanks to store water like home toilets do. They use high-pressure water coming in from a main water pipe instead.

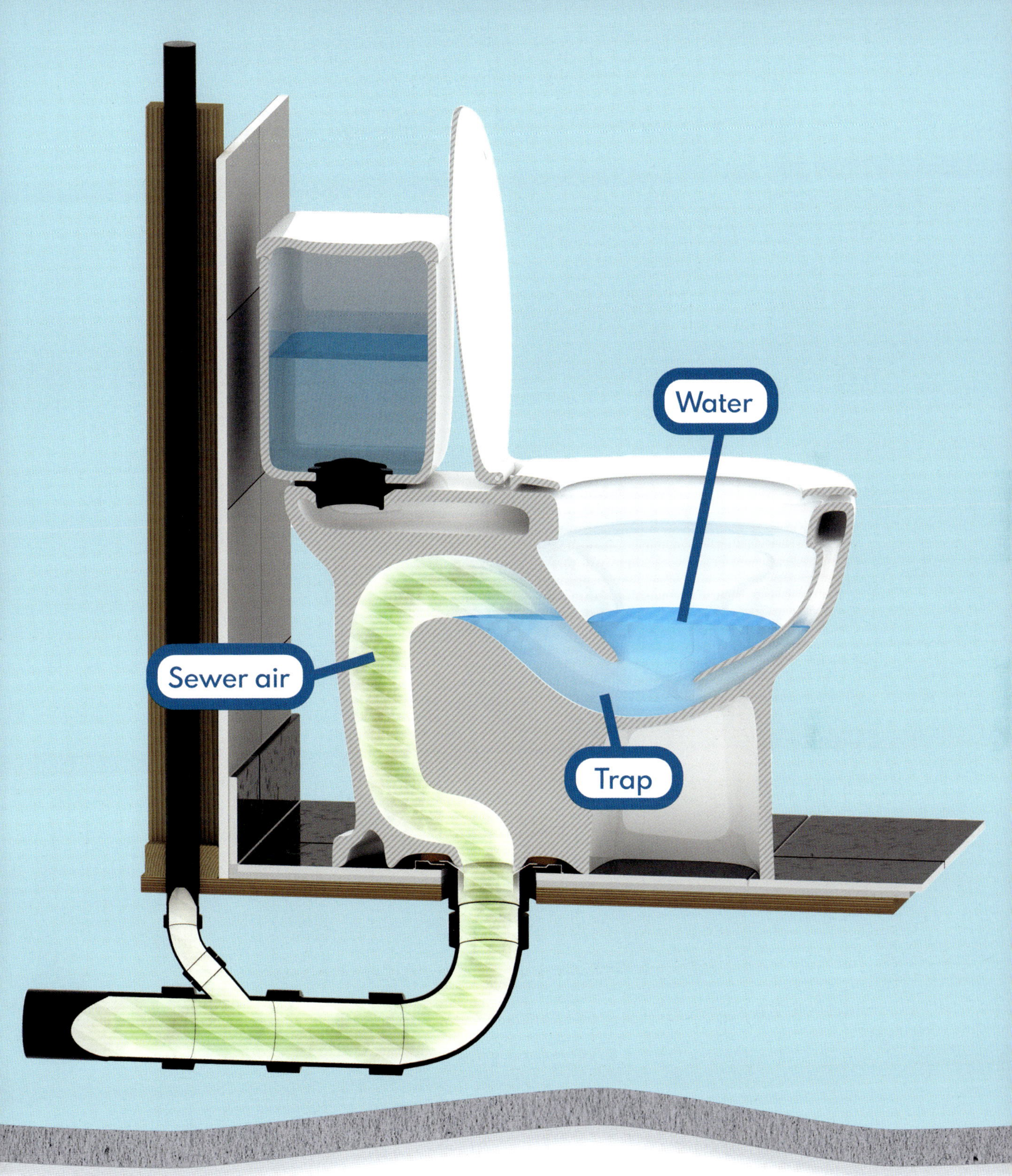

The water inside a toilet's trap acts as a plug. Air from the sewer system cannot escape into the bathroom.

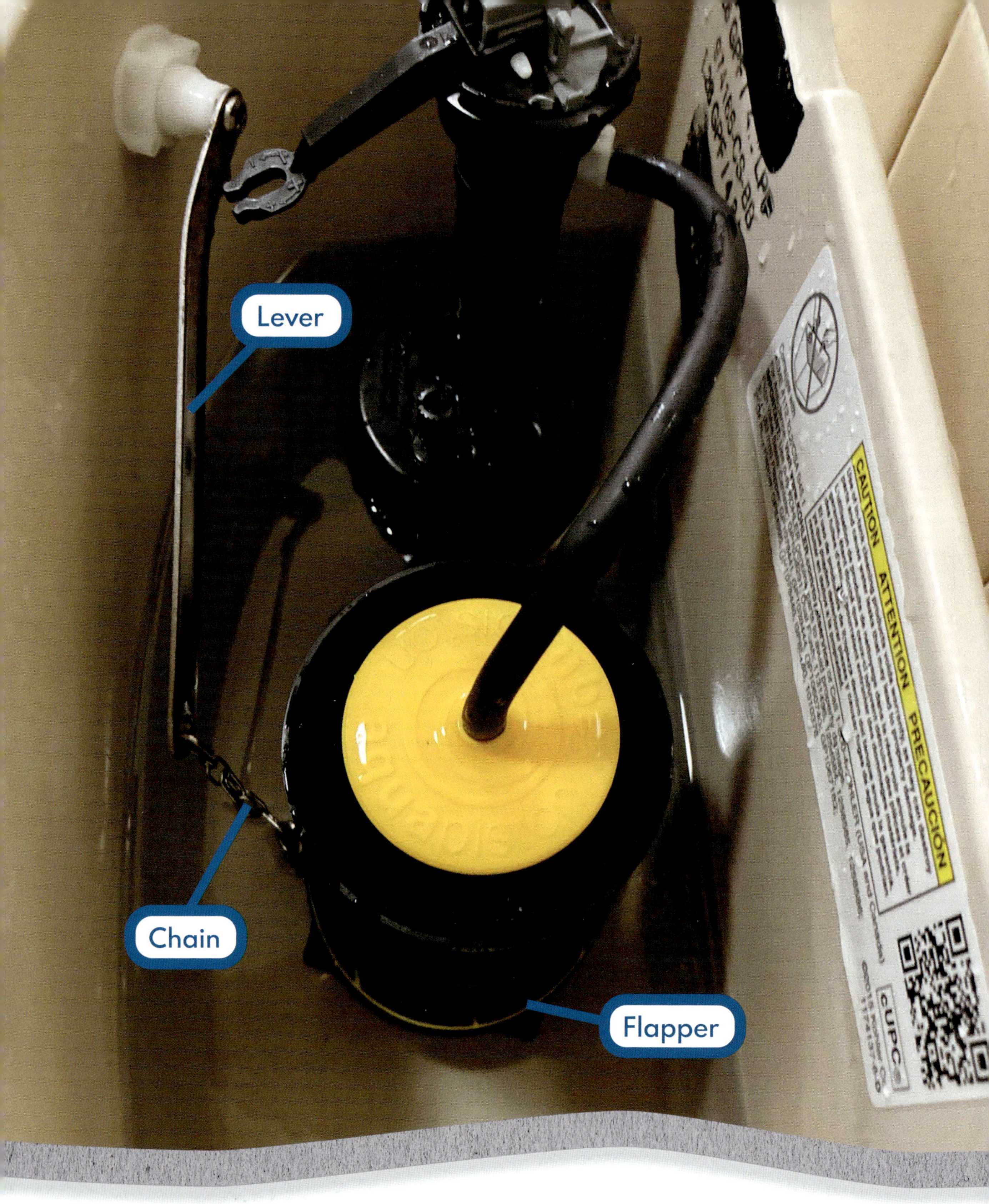

A chain connects the flushing lever to the flapper.

Flush

The time it takes to flush and fill a toilet is short. It usually takes a minute or less. To flush a toilet, a person pushes a lever or button on the tank. The lever connects to a flapper. The flapper is a flat rubber plug. It covers the flush **valve** at the bottom of the toilet tank.

Pushing the lever lifts the flapper. This opens the valve. **Gravity** makes water flow from the tank and through the valve. The valve allows water into the bowl. Water enters the bowl through holes around the top edge of the bowl. These are called rim jets. Water also enters from a **siphon** jet. This is a larger hole near the bottom of the bowl.

Rim jets can get clogged. Regularly cleaning the inside of a toilet helps keep the rim jets working properly.

Rim jets are angled so that water swirls around the bowl. The swirling water moves waste from the bowl into the trap. Water pressure and gravity keep the water and waste moving through the trap and into the sewer system.

When a toilet is flushed, water and waste flow out of the building and toward the sewer system. At the same time, the water in the tank empties into the bowl. Once the tank is empty, the flush valve closes. The flapper shuts the hole from the tank into the bowl.

Further Evidence

Look at the website below. Does it give any new evidence to support Chapter Two?

How Do Toilets Work?

abdocorelibrary.com/toilets-flush-and-fill

People can adjust the height of a ball float so that each flush uses more or less water.

CHAPTER 3

Refilling the Tank

Once a toilet is flushed, water must refill the tank. Inside the tank is a float. Most floats look similar to a sturdy rubber balloon. The float stays on top of the water. It controls the fill valve. This valve lets in fresh water from a pipe connected to the toilet.

When the water level in the tank drops, the float lowers. This opens the fill valve. Water flows into the tank. As the tank fills, the float rises. When the float rises to the proper level, it closes the fill valve. Water stops filling the tank.

The tank also has an overflow tube in case the float or fill valve breaks. This tube keeps the water from rising too high and overflowing the tank. It directs extra water into the bowl.

Other Kinds of Toilets

Modern toilets hold about 1.5 gallons (5.7 L) of water. Older toilets could hold up to 7 gallons (26.4 L) of water. They used a lot of water for each flush.

Flush System

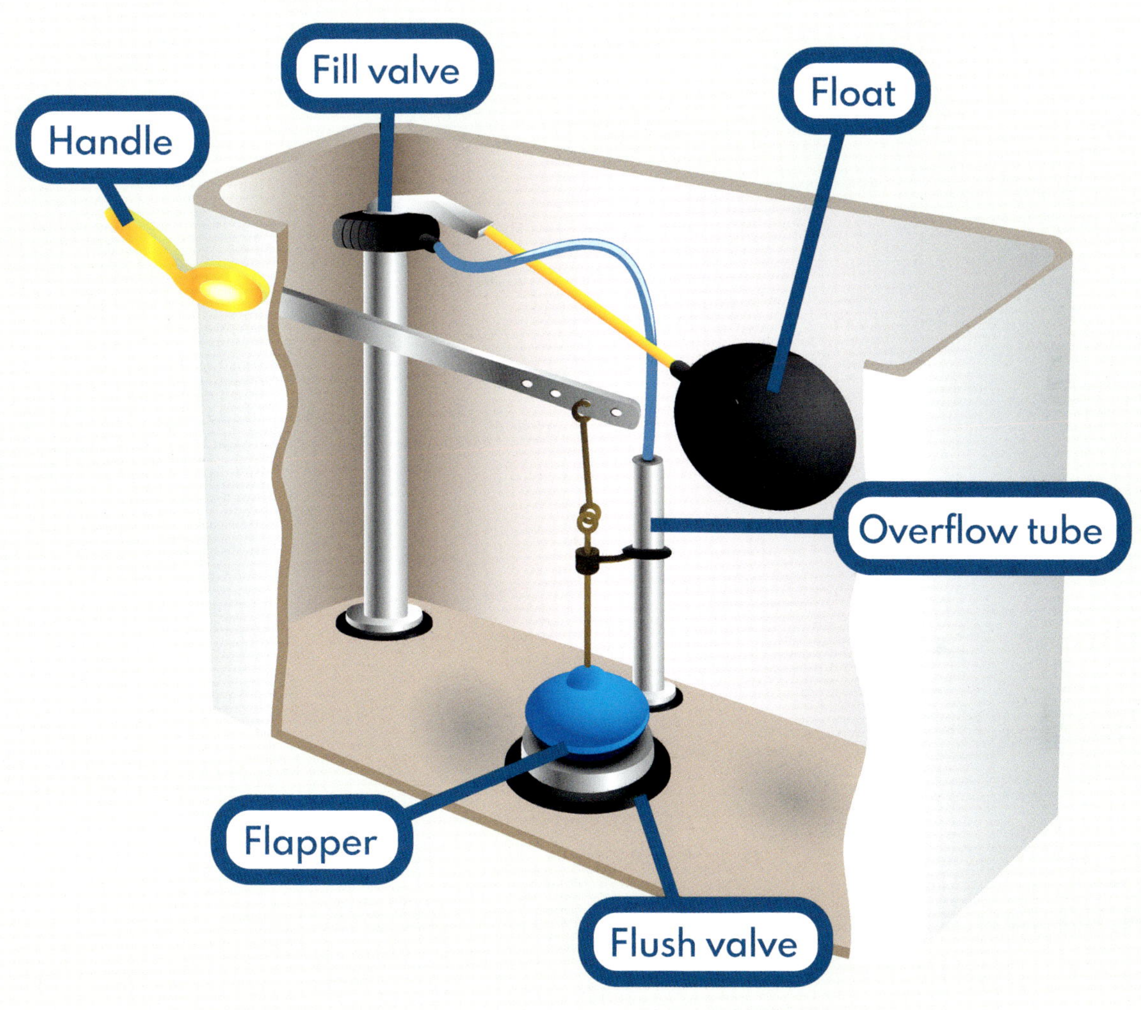

Inside a toilet's tank are parts that help flush away waste. These systems also refill the tank and bowl.

Some toilets have two flush settings. One flush option uses more water than the other. This option is used to flush solid waste.

Using too much water is wasteful. It is bad for the environment. The United States passed laws saying toilets must use less water. So newer toilets are built to flush with less water.

Flushing things other than waste down a vacuum toilet may damage the tank or waste treatment system.

Trains, ships, and planes often use a special kind of toilet called a vacuum toilet. A vacuum toilet uses air and just a small amount of water. It sucks the waste out of the bowl.

Smart Toilets

Smart toilets are now found in some homes. These high-tech toilets offer special features. Possible features include a heated seat, automatic flushing, and a night light.

More than 40 percent of people in the world do not have access to toilets. Health organizations are working to make sure all people can use clean and safe bathrooms.

These toilets empty into tanks. Eventually, the tanks must be emptied. The waste must also be treated.

Toilets use a simple two-step process. They flush and then refill. This important invention makes life cleaner and safer for people.

Explore Online

Visit the website below. Does it give any new information about sewer systems that wasn't in Chapter Three?

How Does a Wastewater Treatment Plant Work?

abdocorelibrary.com/toilets-flush-and-fill

Engineering Facts

The bowl holds water and waste.

The trap keeps water in the bowl and keeps out bad smells.

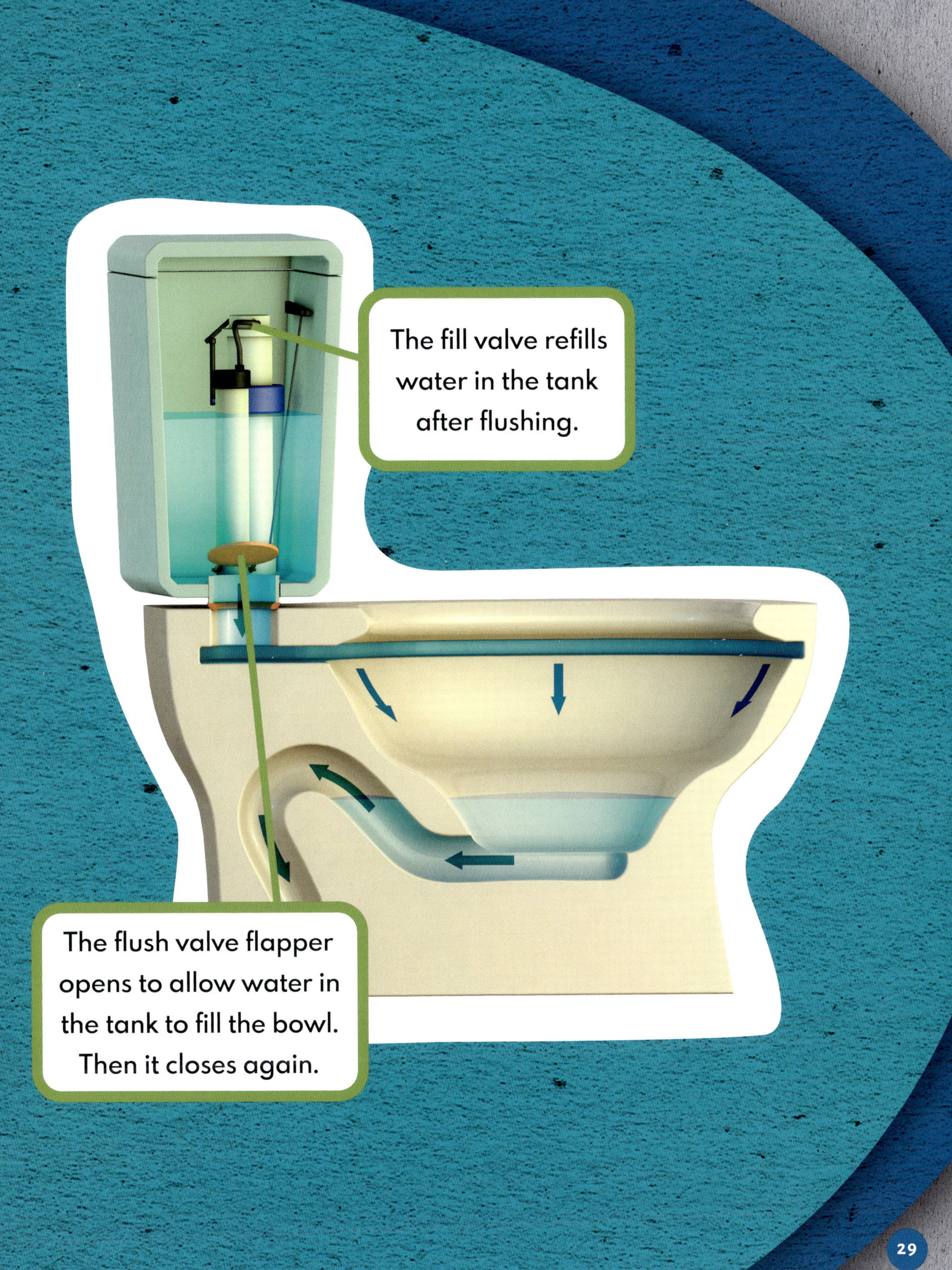
The fill valve refills water in the tank after flushing.
The flush valve flapper opens to allow water in the tank to fill the bowl. Then it closes again.

Glossary

clog
to block movement through a pipe

engineers
people who are trained to design and build machines and structures

gravity
the force that pulls things down to the ground

sewage
solid and liquid waste

sewer system
pipes and pumps that carry sewage away from homes, schools, and businesses for it to be treated

siphon
a bent pipe that moves a liquid from one container to another using air pressure

valve
a device that controls the flow of a liquid through a pipe

Online Resources

To learn more about toilets, visit our free resource websites below.

Visit **abdocorelibrary.com** or scan this QR code for free Common Core resources for teachers and students, including vetted activities, multimedia, and booklinks, for deeper subject comprehension.

Visit **abdobooklinks.com** or scan this QR code for free additional online weblinks for further learning. These links are routinely monitored and updated to provide the most current information available.

Learn More

Murray, Julie. *Toilet*. Abdo, 2023.

Paeff, Colleen. *The Great Stink*. Margaret K. McElderry Books, 2021.

Ventura, Marne. *How Dams Hold Back Water*. Abdo, 2025.

Index

About the Author

Donna B. McKinney is the author of more than 25 nonfiction books for kids. Her debut picture book *LIGHTS ON! Glow-in-the-Dark Deep Ocean Creatures* released in 2023. Before she wrote for children, McKinney spent many years writing about science and technology topics such as chemistry, space science and robotics at the US Naval Research Laboratory in Washington, DC. She lives in North Carolina.